CW00867697

This collection of poetry is forever dedicated to the best, furriest friend I have ever had. He goes by many names:

The Sheriff

Hunter Bunter Boo

Bubba

Hunty

He was a best friend. He adored his mother and loved his aunties. He was a true gentleman who knew his way around the kitchen, picking up any fallen scraps and occasionally begging for some if he couldn't find any.

He was the cherished brother of Holly, Finn and Rosie. But being cherished wasn't always easy. He had to quickly assume the necessary duty of SHERIFF. Maintaining order among the four four-legged friends was becoming crucial and Hunter, being the most qualified, excelled at his new job!

Although stressful and tiring, he never took a day off. He was truly the BEST BOY!

Rest in paradise Bubba, we love you forever!

The Poetry Kitchen

All work written, edited and owned by
Brendan De Lucia
Published by Blurb
All rights reserved
Copyright 2021

Illustrations and Cover Font
Gordon Johnson via Pixabay
Cover script font provided by Koen van der Bliek

Created in the United States of America

Other titles by Brendan De Lucia:
Page Publishing Poetry Anthology: Volume 1
Absinthe | Poetry Novel
Grilled Cheese & Whiskey | Poetry Novel
Behind the Dumpster | Poetry Novel

Brendan De Lucia

The Poetry Kitchen

A collection of Poems and Short Stories

The Poetry Kitchen

Brendan De Lucia

Prologue

Trolls are Inherently Rich

Said the widow
who's apparently
a witch.

Her husband,
the late sorcerer,
was once a torturer
who would torture her.

One day she
slashed his throat,
yet no one cried
murderer!

His body was brought
to a pair of connected bridges,
where our widow awaited
her freedom and riches.

The obese beasts bared
their teeth and opened
their stomachs.
The riddance
of evil is a
fortune we
all must
covet.

Brendan De Lucia

The Poetry Kitchen

Part One

Man and Beast

- Foul Kiss

Milk white fangs sank their feet
deep into my nape while pale lips
whispered into my ear.
At first I was weak,
for a glorious voice
was all I could hear.

Accepting the pain,
I could feel teeth on bone.
Floating into black, the faceless
voice began to moan.

Then my heart bloomed,
reminding me of my power.
I must not allow this evil
to acquire this flower...

...committing to self-love,
my blood quickly became toxic.
The fangs retracted and
the voice lost its logic.

My life drew swords
with the legions
of my own
hellacious
abyss.

Freeing my soul
from such a

lovely, foul kiss.

-Plant Love

Falling for you
felt as natural as
the leaves in autumn.
Sinking with speed,
my toes touched the sands
of your heart's ocean bottom.
Using both feet, I was able to plant love
where it has been long forgotten.
I waited a moment, then swam
to the surface just in time
to watch it blossom.

- Standing in The Ocean

I used to board my windows
with splinters so the winters
wouldn't be able to infiltrate.
My bones were fragile.
The chill was agile.
I was simply trying
to meditate.

I was overwhelmingly sad.
Drinking, smoking,
and listening to jazz.

Yet, optimistic for sunshine.
So I put down the moonshine,
walked the shoreline and
followed the moon's shine.

Standing in the ocean,
your figure rolled with the waves.
Before I could drown,
I knew I was saved.

-Path

I don't miss the overflowing wastebasket
brimming with bloody band-aids
from finger wounds caused by
broken guitar strings.
You've brought the music,
so I'll stick with the words
and untying our shoe strings.
Two barefoot lovers dancing
around a depleted bonfire.
Two trees in heat blazing
an uncontrollable wildfire.
You've completed my math.
You, are my path.

- Weather Whether

Begging the ancient ones for wisdom,
I found myself in a vulnerable position.

Exposing my need for desire, I became
unaware of the skeletons stoking my fire.

Feeling my flesh melt, I could sense
my demons reaching out.

I wished for rain and willed
the weather to oblige.
Watering the flames
making steam burn the sky.

There's always a price,
whether you can or can't afford it.
But he moral question remains the
same, is it truly worth it?

- Plastic Pistols

I don't miss
screaming at the silence.
Nor live streaming domestic violence.

(My white noise was carnage)

Loaded plastic pistols
protected my dreams
from plagued pirates and
camouflaged elected officials.

(Wickedness incarnate)

My freedom was being
challenged by racism.
Hope was pursued
by journalism.
Truth, interpreted
through terrorism.
I look forward to investing in
defense mechanisms as a way to
defend all of Earth's living organisms.

- Postcard Sunset

You can outline my darkness
by picturing me as a silhouette,
and if you look hard enough
you can feel the sunrise
of a postcard sunset.

But don't forget,

You can't spell I Love You
without aid from the alphabet.
Because without words or pictures,
we individually resemble the shapes
of marionettes.

- FUN

We have become obsessed
with government renovation,
causing increased human segregation.
We, the people, should be obsessed
with interspecies innovation
and prolonging mortality's
desolation.
It's not
too late
to undo
what's been done.
Spreading hatred is easy.

Spreading love will be fun.

- changing

Soggy leaves
leave behind
the residue of autumn.
Fertilizing summer's soil
so the winter snowflakes
can blossom.

- Mud Stuck

Lions act on instinct
and sharks follow their stomachs.
Humans run on soft drinks
and time plays tricks with puppets.
Lovers devour passion.
Vampires suck blood.
Vote for compassion.
Get stuck in some mud.

- Simple Communication

Stars
get lonely too,
so they've adapted illumination.

A simple form of intimacy,
like human communication.

- Shock Therapy

I used to follow the
power lines home
and chase lightning
down to the dock.
I've been Electrocuted
so many times I am now
immune to the shock.
Now I hunt for food
and toothpicks.
The combination,
plus you, produces
perfect acoustics.

It's shockingly therapeutic.

- Stained Glass Clouds

Three dimensional clouds
remind me of your rosy cheeks
pressed against twilight pillows.
The same way your
eyes remind me
of stained glass
windows.

- High Success

Heartbeats
listen better
than eardrums.

That's why
communicating with love
has a higher success rate.

- Fireworks & S'mores

I want to live
off the land
inside of your
imagination.
I want to be the king
of your wilderness
and the cup you
steep your
coffee in.
I want to
show you how
fire works outdoors.
I just want to be your
fireworks and s'mores.

\- Flip

A relationship
is a thread that
must not strip.
A kiss is a grip
that must not slip.
Sex is a section
you must not skip.
Love is a ship
you must
not flip.

- Saffron Fingers

His finger tips
tickled the petals
of wild saffron flowers.
Plucking a few filaments
to spice up their love life.

- Beach Chair

I am
addicted
to the way
Atlantic seashells
dangle around your neck.
I love the way you walk around
barefoot on the sun-burnt deck.
You have power and I have proof.
You're the best part of any vacation.
You're the beer equipped
beach chair up on the roof.

- Awesome Blossom

Life is a front yard garden
and love is a seed in the sun.
We humans are the plants
waiting to see which
flower we become.

- Lettuce

Pursue someone
who pursues dreams.
Stop pursuing someone
who sells them.

Fight for someone
who will massage
your feet and
humorously
smell them.

Fall for someone
who can get lettuce
stuck in their teeth
and laughs when
you tell them.

-Pressured Relationships

Words have spines
that can be bent
with pressure.
If they hold,
your message will
contain adventure.
If they snap, then the words
were never meant to be together.

- Fenway

You remind me
of narrow streets in Italy.

The old ones with the bicycles.

You remind me
of beaches in July.
The warm ones
with sunshine
and Popsicles.

You remind me
of moonshine.
Both cosmic
and alcoholic.

You remind me of Caroline,
Fenway's sweetest narcotic.

- Salted Death

You
are like
the oceans,
filled with life.
Infinite potential.
Beautifully mysterious.
Dangerously consuming.
I no longer fear drowning.
I wish to die at sea.

- Guidance

Dry those eyes with this smile.
Embrace your bones with my arms.
Lift up your chin with these fingers.
Use my fists to fight off your enemies.
Use my feet keep moving forward.
Allow my love to guide you home.

- Midnight Lick

Melt into my bowl of ice cream
so I can consume you as
my midnight snack.
I promise to lick
the spoon and
eventually
melt you
back.

- Foodie

Exquisite taste
radiates from the
caramel pupils of her
chocolate eyes. A couple
of oven roasted pecan pies.
She has a bewitching smile and
baked goods consume her sugary
lifestyle. Cinnamon apple skin makes
my mouth water and drip from my chin.

✻

Does she taste like dessert?
I've daydreamed too many hours
about those red velvet lips.
It's disgusting what
I would do for her
red velvet
kiss.

- Laughing Snow

Snowflakes in wind are at the will
of their surroundings. Constants
of nature constantly drowning.
Be like the human. A
consistent variable.
Unpredictability
makes life
hysterical.

- Exposed Temptation

Let's strip down until we expose our flesh.
Entangle our bones and hold our breath.
Tease our hearts, flirt with death.
Lick our lips and bite our necks.
Provoke temptation with
fingers and tongues,
fuck until the sun
makes both
of us come.

- Internal Vibrations

Excitement,
allows the heart
to anticipate.

To flutter, to quake,
to shiver, to palpitate.

Anticipation,
requires internal alignment.
Long life is the product
of eternal excitement.

- Possessed

Skeletons
haunt my
daydreams.

A sick trick
to embody
the fleshy
monsters of
my nightmares.

- Lost Wonder

Black and white reflections
prove that the world
around us is filled
with color.

Reflections
remain constant.
Life remains a wonder.

- Drug of Choice

You
are the
Celestite crystal
vibrating my mahogany
mantel above a brick fireplace.
Energizing the birch smoke,
causing blue ash clouds
to crystallize as resin
on the bookcase.
My drug of choice
when needing to
resort my
delusive
heart to
its illusive
hiding place.

- Dragon Pearls

Dear troublemaker,
your soul has more
depth than the
graves of an
underwater
undertaker.

That "dragon hide"
of yours is really just sand,
you chestnut-eyed glass-maker.

I see no shell.
Only one remarkable seashell.
You saguaro pearl-maker.

- Matrix of Death

Wet powder
caused a failed
assassination.
Dry flowers die
due to lack of
hydration.
Nature saves.
Nature kills.
Nature lacks
behavioral skills.

-Hungry Love

Love must be as random as nature.
It must never be advertised
or categorized.
Once satisfied,
no longer
does it
appear
beautiful
and blooming,
but dangerous
and consuming.

- Physics

You're my moon.
My constant within
this kaleidoscope universe
of infinite variables.

- ...savior loading...

...I see you ...

...floating in opal brine...

...I would love to save you
if you let me cast a line...

- Up the Rabbit Hole

Nature,
runs on sunlight
and abides by moon phases.
I long to be as happy as the
Hare that moon gazes.

- Ambition

Tell a human "it's impossible"
and watch the world shrink.
Evolution is expansion.
Fewer limits.
Nearer brinks.

- Wastebasket

I loved you once,
on jumbled sheets of flavor.
Until the sunrise illuminated
the wastebasket, reminding me
that you're only neatly crumpled
pieces of paper.

- Drunk Sexting...I mean Texting*

"Love is a frontier adventure"

Was plastered across
the patient pamphlets.
Certificates adorned the walls
but the plaques were all slanted.
You see, I crossed the line,
so my therapist decided
to drug test me.
...
I just really
wanted you
to drunk text me.

- Hitchhiking Knight

Step inside a lie and watch
how the blood flows true.
Pearly white doors await
the flow to pass through.
Lanterns glow white.
Flames burn blue.
A lie is knight
on a quest
to be viewed.

- Bottomless Happiness

Remember your value.
Showcase your worth.
Life moves too fast to
succumb to anything
short of constant,
unrelenting happiness.
The depths of comfortability
for the sake of pleasing
outside opinions
is bottomless.

- Bare Necessities

The bare minimum is often
everything you need.
Sunshine, dreams
and a belly to feed.

- Opal Magic

I am a hopeful romantic.
Hopelessly clinging to
opal enchantments.

- Cosmic Connections

Stars
explode
so humans
can cast wishes.
For tales to be told,
death must build bridges.

- Scarlet Fever

She was
a lover of poetry.
A beautiful believer.
Then she read mine and
succumbed to a fever.
Our romance was severed,
fingerprints on the cleaver.
I have read my words too,
I wouldn't date me either.

Brendan De Lucia

- 60

I want to be sixty
with a pantry
full of food,
shelves full
of books and
decanters
of whiskey.
Rooms filled
with grandkids,
cameras for candids
and a dog to miss me.
I just want to be sixty
with whiskey and a wife
to kiss me.

- Popsicles

Be like the witty,
shitty wisdom on
sticky Popsicle sticks
and make somebody smile.

- Burn Cold

Adventure
brings out the
rainbows in your soul.
Stars imitate your eyes
which burn brighter
than the moon
when it's whole.

Hearts are warm.

Skin is cold.

Love is young.

Life is old.

- Kiss me in the rain

I want to melt your heart,
but I refuse to cause
you pain.
So I'll let you
melt mine
if you promise
to kiss me in the rain.

- Trolls

I kissed you once
and you gave me
money for tolls.
To bribe the
horny trolls
who traffic
lonely souls.

- Moments

Life is about living in the moment.
Except for when that moment
jeopardizes the possibility of
future moments.

- Prisoner

Bodies grow old with age.
Souls are eternal, waiting
for death to unlock the cage.

- Year 3021

Although the world
seems flooded with
fearful tears,
the sun
will continue
to rise for at least
a thousand more years.

- Simple Beauty

The simplest
forms are always
the most beautiful.
Complexity aside,
you are simply
so beautiful.

- Souvenir

I kept you like a souvenir
on the wall in a sports bar.
Similar to that picture you
keep hidden inside of your
sports bra.

- Dying Kiss

You claim to be
a fatal craving
and I'm addicted
to death.

The dead can vouch,
I would kill to kiss you
with my last breath.

-Piece of Art

The day I go missing
will be the day you'll
find me in your heart.
Our masterpiece may drip,

but we will always be
my favorite
piece of art.

- Patient Volcano

You're an
active volcano.
Surrounded by
emerald waterfalls,
spewing stars of gold.
You, are an antique adventure
awaiting patiently to be told.

- Paranormal

I was the hangman
at my own hanging.
A ghost reborn
to the sounds
of commercial
branding.

- Anchor Ring

Your face
is my everything.

A sun.
A moon.
The stars
and oceans.
Your face is my
anchor ring.

- Candy Eyes

Your eyes,
mint green.
Skin as decadent
as French cream.
Hair, the color brandy.
Lips, soft, sweet and tangy.
My mistake, thinking your heart
was a piece of candy.

- Manifest Memory

In life, use imagination
to manifest memory.
Because in death,
we seek to forever
re-live memories.

- Scarred Stars

When I am
beneath you
I am under the
protection of shiny stars.
Locations of constellations
match the placements of each
of our tiny scars.

- Looking Back is Sexy

Stop chasing people
who don't periodically
look back to see if you're
still chasing them.

-TWO PLUS TWO

Man in mask.
Lady in black.
Lies and facts.
Lie in cracks.
Back to back.
The lion reacts.
Face to face.
We both collapse.

- Equals Four

I used to hate sleeping alone.

My voids were so big,
I was never so wrong.

I am never alone.
Body and soul.

It's a two seater rig.

Love,
it's a two
person gig.

- Apples & Sex

It was great sex under a full moon.
A gravitational anomaly in mid June.
Two roses of winter abloom.
Apples of fire
completely
consumed.

- A Perfect Poop

Let mistakes remind you
that perfection is overrated.
Trying to always be perfect
is like always being
constipated.

- Aquatic Librarians

You remind me
of field trips to
the aquarium...
and
...sneaking into
libraries to piss off
the old librarians.

- Fire & Mead

She is magic.
He needed glasses.
They were fabric.
Booze and matches.

- Science Class

I broke down the word DISTANCE

and discovered LOVE was still existent.

I deciphered the mystery of MILES
and realized measurements are

breadcrumbs shaped like SMILES.

I dissected the rituals of SPACE
and observed how separation
cannot displace.

Long story short,

if it's REAL it's REAL.

- Just a Dream

The thought of your curves
helps me dream away the pain
of your curves only being a thought.

- She Wolf

You are wild.
A wolf in winter.
Red paw prints.
Fresh kills.
Freethinker.
Cruel as hunger.
Maternal lover.
Soft as slumber.
Mortal mother.

- Moon Mirror

That smile.
An infection.
Earths greatest
invention.
That heart.
Those eyes.
The moon's
greatest
reflection.

- Memory Error

I was the update your phone
didn't have enough space
to download.

-100 Years

You are a full moon
in my rear view mirror.
A flash fire epiphany.

Your past will
always be beautiful.
So go ahead and move on.
You have just about a century.

- Power Couple

I am stronger than I look...

...so maybe this time
you don't have
to heal alone.

- Stuck in the Rain

I have
finally accepted
the simplicity of happiness.

It's the sound of rain.
It's the thought of you smiling
between the same rain drops as I.
It's being stuck in the same rain
underneath the same sky.

- Sweet, sweet Love

Soft piano.
Quite crackling
from the fireplace
dying across the room.
Shadows making love along the walls.
Lost deposits, broken furniture,
alcohol and unknown narcotics.
Two cold bodies in the bed.
White sheets stained.
Hearts weak.
Love made.
So sweet.

– Dream Jumping

Ah, cliffs.
The view.
The wind.
The birds.
The waves.
The stars.
The moon.
The fall.
The rocks.
The fish.
My doom.

The Poetry Kitchen

Part Two

Lost at Sea

- Commandeer

We snuck aboard
like proper pirates.
Struck a bargain with a
crow with a copper iris.
Tiptoed the planks to avoid
waking sleeping giants.
Ventured below deck
to escape the climate.
Smuggled rum from
the brig to the
privacy of the
captain's quarters.
Drank until the sunset
and sunrise were over.

- Genie in a whiskey bottle

I wish I could run barefoot
through jade meadows
of storybook fairy-tales.
Catch happy raindrops with
sand-made pails, gather gravity
in backpacks and harness the
wind with handmade sails.
Stash away solid bars of earth
inside of golden fishtanks.
Walk across the water
upon the waves of
frozen riverbanks.
I wish I could wake up
somewhere far away.
A spiritual bouquet.
With someone
I can love
everyday.

-A Jar named Mason

Splinters have pierced my stomach due
to termites feasting on my heart.
It was whittled from old
oak whiskey barrels,
a true piece of art.
Soaked in blood,
the burgundy
sawdust
relieves any
appetite for love.
Reinforced with steel,
I shall repel the invaders.
Slowly I will heal, fermenting into
oblivion inside of mason jar containers.

- Therapy

I am a whiskey bottle,
negligently seeping my
fermented emotions.
I am a frisky novel,
viciously scheming

sex-scented explosions.

I am a crispy waffle,
bleeding bourbon

blended devotion.

I am a gypsy fossil,
desperately feeding on

the tormented oceans.

I am salty and stressed.
Trapped inside of
a fishy brothel,

awaiting implosion.

- WAR

People label me as strange.
Pointing fingers and waving suggestions.
Forming lines in alphabetical processions.
Asking rhetorical and hypothetical questions.
I am a complex human with simple obsessions.
An emotional wreck with countless confessions.
I confess I am obsessed with making impressions.
It is a formidable weapon against the war of

depression.

- Master of Life

Governed by the moon,
It touches the sky and
swallows the sun.
Mother of monsters.
Collector of souls.
Master of life.
Impossibly old.
Reborn each sunrise,
when the pearly brine
licks the peachy sand.
The sea is home.
The soul of all
whom walk
on land.

- Damaged Photographs

The love I yearn for is ancient.
Yet relatively young and patient.
It hibernates between the grains
of damaged photographs.
Concealing its location
within the synopsis
paragraphs.
Water marks
act as the cipher.
Submerged answers
revealed by legions of fire.
Illumination guides my heart
home, back to sandy shores.
Where the love I yearn for
awaits my soul with
open arms of war.

- Courting by Fire

I tried breaking
into your rigged heart
with heart-shaped dynamite.
My explosives mated with yours,
creating an unbearable Fahrenheit.
We let the flames melt our flesh to bone.
Allowing the smoke to guide our
entangled souls home.

- Literature

Love,
is like
writing
a novel.

It starts with a prologue.
An introduction to trauma.
A comedic tragedy, balanced
by action and drama.

Characters develop.

Along with trust
and an anticipation
of striking gold.

A climactic testament
of commitment
ending with your
story being
told.

-Tangerine Death

Tree bark for skin.
We are jungle trees of sin.
Addicted to evil
and solitary spaces.
Momentary stars.
Medieval places.
Silhouettes singed against
tangerine skies.
Cigarette breath.
Nicotine lies.
Dressed to depress.
Everybody cries.
Internet death.
Tambourine eyes.

- Autumn

Her maple
hair matches the
autumn highway foliage
which matches her flannel shirt.
Lips taste like caramel apple
cider donuts, pumpkin pie
and lemon sherbet.

- Crime Scene

I look for your face in raindrops.
Search for your taste in gumdrops.
Track your scent to bus stops.
Follow you home by gunshots.
Except the rain was acid.
The candy was poisoned.
Your perfume was stale
and the bullet casings
were missing.

- Mammoth killer

Quivering in fear,
the mighty mammoth
knelt before me, pledging service.
For I killed the beast who hunts the mammoth.
Exerting dominance I found my purpose.
Shivering in hypothermic waters,
mortally freezing its spine, the
great Bengal tiger waited
as I hunted to kill time.
Picnics in the heart
of the savanna,
because the
coalitions
have been
defused.
The lions
were run
underground,
hounded and abused.
Man is absolute, in this sick game
of life and chance. We, the human,
the ultimate weapon of destruction,
do a little dance and await
the world's eruption.

- Snowflakes

Life is moving.
Death is coming.
We are all snowflakes.
Spontaneously spiraling
through life's realm of
free will until we meet
our fate's final end.

- Stratosphere

Violet dawn skies savor
all of our classified secrets.
Violent midsummer sunrises
favor all of our magnified uniqueness.
Bonfires consume the air and mate the aromas
into euphoric, airborne addictions.
Campfires harbor the rare and
mandate that tequila shots
forewarn questionable
decisions.
Long nights
end once the
morning sunlight
infiltrates the atmosphere.
Strobe lights and spaceships
guide us home like satellites
through the stratosphere.

-Alexandria

Gunshots and steel blades have carved out
the sounds and bloody pathways of the past.
A closer look will show you how death
is necessary for short-term power when
all life moves fast. Be warned. These roads
are off-limits, you must quickly interpret
then improvise. Your own life you must
unravel, lift the damned curse and crystallize.
Adapt rare characteristics known for causing
phenomenal, groundbreaking and marvelous
earthquakes. Set sail for glory without ever
forgetting your birth place. How do you
achieve the legend of sitting in an
Alexandrian bookcase?

Dance with the devil.
Beat time in a foot race.

\- *Alice*

Golden handles
provide routes of passage
to diamond crusted universes.
Ruby red skylines supply dreams
of passion and unsung freedom verses.
Silently shimmering silver lakes reflect
the creation of life's odyssey. Daylight quietly
quivers away, disconnecting in preparation for
night's prophecy. The only vegetation in
abundance is copper-tone cacti. The
proper presentation instructed is
white suits and proper sown
black ties. The deep hue
of the shadow casted
by the nomadic cacti
palace, veiled the
rabbit-hole in
which I fell
through to
find my way

to *Alice.*

- Birds Chirp

It was 6am in Boston.
Spring morning, windows open.
The sunrise was act one.
Followed by act two:
The trancing
early traffic.

Coffee bean aroma
filled the city air.
Hints of strawberries,
vanilla, honey and pear.

Past the market and beyond the
bustling streets. I honed in to the
river orchestra of musical fleets.
Act three:
Birds chirping their
morning renditions.
Then I awoke.
Succumbing.
Listening.

- Bloody Mailbox

Handcuffed to the persuasions of reality
television. The common human falls victim
to absolute despotism. The media King who
inspires controlled chaos, was granted the ax
to the kingdom shortly after the devil was paid
off. Meetings in secret and blood pacts forged in
gunpowder, this ruthless ruler burned down
the empire with toxic roses and sunflowers.
With the assistance of fear, his loyal subjects
dressed in their best bronze robes and jail
socks. Every home in the nation flew a
black flag, cut grass and
bloody mailbox.

- Decisions

Buried
beneath
thick layers
of spellbinding
indecision, dwells the
building blocks of intuition.
Go against the ripples if the currents
appear false. Invite in fear for dinner and
then together dance the Waltz. Eye to eye
these devils are only ghosts. You, must decide
for yourself which path you want to walk the most.

- Desires

I desire to be
a world traveler.
A lost wanderer.
A curious adventurer.
A wide-eyed explorer.
A friendly migrant.
A fate led navigator.
A born sailor.
A romantic daredevil.
An opportunistic pirate.
A driven pioneer.
A displaced outcast
on a pilgrimage.
A trailblazing nomad.
A hitchhiking tourist.
An alien rover
exploring foreign lands
simply desiring all
there is to see.

- Sullied Kings

The time has come to unmask the chieftains.
Publicize propaganda and unearth the heathens.
When righteous men seamlessly corrupt their
ethical philosophies, spineless pens illustrate
theoretical and unethical prophecies.
Rich with tampered power fueled
by manipulative greed.
These evil kings must
all face disgrace.
Banish them
cruelly or
turn
them
to feed.
They express
fear just the same.

They cower. They bleed.

-Jaws

I once read a book
about a journey to the
center of the Earth. So I
embarked on a daring voyage
to discover the true origin of our birth.
The black words on the white pages became my
heading while the binding transfigured into
the vessel for my imagination. With no idea
where I was heading, I was stubborn in
finding the temple at the absolute
center of gravitation. I needed to
make sure I was still alive.
I needed to make sure
that when I closed
my eyes I could
still fly.
I needed
to feel the thrill
of never coming home.
I needed to be bit by the

jaws of the unknown.

- Cozy Paradise

Once paradise
becomes a state of mind,
you're free to roam the universe
without bubbles and their cozy confines.

-Jewels

Sapphire and Ruby
whisper in secret
under the protection
of a diamond night sky.
Dawn after dawn,
Dusk flirts with
Amber and Aquamarine
while the fireflies fly.
Ivory and Jade
are frequently spotted
walking the beach with
Pearl and Moonstone.
Mr. Onyx resides underground
with Gold and Tombstone.
Rose Quartz left behind
distinct footprints which
lead to Earth's heart.
Where my hunt for the
incomparable gem stones
shall end and start.

- Leaf

Hello leaf.
Soulless and free.
How on Earth did
you manage to find
all of this solace in me?
From where have you come?
Please, tell me your name.
Such travel is menacing.
I can see you brimming
with pain.
Vipers wait.
Hidden yet watching.
The roads you require
are treacherous and daunting.

Goodbye leaf.
Soulless and free.
Here is an eye to see
all that you see.
Goodbye leaf.
Forever at peace.
You've opened my mind
to a life truly free.

- Meals

Breakfast with presidents of exotic islands
uncharted. The coffee is hot and all threats
have been bombarded. Brunch with queens
in shadow with their pet crows as witness. The
tea is hot, steeped with blood to enhance the
richness. Lunch with family friends at
12pm sharp. There will be sandwiches,
burgers, chicken and carp. Dinner
will be served with thieves
to discuss their next
great heist. Except
the food has all
disappeared,
as well
as the ice.
Dessert will be
with my enemies,
to resolve and renew.
Our guns will be unloaded

as our differences settle over Tiramisu.

- Momentum

High velocity asteroids
terrorize without exception.
I must observe their trajectory
on my odyssey to redemption.
If symptoms begin to emerge,
the only medicine is no medicine.
Into a black hole I must submerge.

Body and mind.
Soul and skeleton.

The answers I seek
inhabit intrinsic dimensions.
The aliens I trade with for habit,
acquire intrinsic deception. They
will attempt to derail me with
irrational impressions. I must
remember the characteristics
of the asteroid and never
lose my momentum.

- Oblivion

Blind pilots taught me how
to fly the skies with closed eyes.
Devoted pirates taught me how to
disguise the spies with composed lies.
I was piss drunk in the vineyards of Eden,
smoking pot and eating apples. Taking shots
with demons, hunting wolves and eating jackals.
Beer in hand, I mounted the barely balancing
banisters hovering over the blackness. Double
fisting mixed drinks, I welcomed oblivion.
Embracing the madness.

- Piano & Guitar

Becoming bored of bathtubs,
I decided to transition to
bathing in meteor showers.
After getting bored of back rubs,
I decided to shoot handguns at
the backs of greedier powers.
We exist solely to be the
seeds to replenish
intelligent life.
Instructed to
sow the
Earth
and cut down
the irrelevant with
an intelligent knife.
So when the planet starts
to die and the fiascoes turn bizarre.
You'll find me by the campfire, drunk
and high with a piano and guitar.

- Subway Rides

I took the midnight subway into the city.
The conductor, myself and a stranger
around fifty. Jazz on the intercom.
Faint scents of lemon balm.
Pulled fire alarms and
loaded firearms.

- A Cappella Birds

Life
should be
about examining
the beauty of listening
to the morning conversations
of those radioactive,
a cappella birds.
They speak
in secret
tongues
of ancient
mysteries,
telling stories
without words.

- Forgetful

When winter winds
intimately invade
the transcendent
summer sunshine.
I feel free from
emotions entangling
me in mephitic moonshine.
The shivering subtly
overwhelms the sweat,
allowing acidic alchemy
to sober my emotions
and help forget.

- Sexy Traits

Ambitious hearts
don't have time to
tolerate laziness.
Fear is psychological.
A product of undisciplined craziness.
A dedicated mind
is the sexiest trait
we humans radiate.
Love is only true when
both heart and mind
learn how to communicate.

- Horny Weather

I don't want that tinder type of love
brightening my days during
horny, stormy weather.
I want the random
kind of love that
settles after the
storm passes,
lasting
forever.

- Nude Lover

I want a house by the sea.
With a telescope for stars
fastened to the floor of
the second floor balcony.
A study full of typewriters
and a lab to practice alchemy.
Chimney full of fire.
Kitchen full of food.
A bed full of love
with my lover
fully nude.

- City Hares

Making awkward eye contact
with two furry rabbits,
I instantly felt guilty
swallowing my last
bite of roasted
carrots.

- Zombie Voodoo

The detectives said
it was a murder of two.
The coroner confirmed
it was NOT death by flu.
Autopsies revealed that their hearts
had rusty screws pierced straight through.
The lawyers wanted 1st degree and
continued to pursue. So I killed
for love, becoming a zombie
operator of voodoo. I then
pleaded guilty, bid adieu
and told the judge
my motive
was you.

-1,000 Fathoms

Atlantic winds whisper secrets
of European adventures.
Sea creatures babble
on about the swanky
underwater architecture.
Foreign salts exfoliate
my American skin tan.
I am a realistic
daydreamer
with a
very
real
imaginary wingspan.

I want to be the fly
on your wallflower.

- Painted Thieves

Your heart
is a dye pack
of actual blood.
Exploding on the
unworthy thieves
attempting to claim
your riches as
their own.

- Cremation Station

Once you learn the art
of cremating the past.
Your future will be rid
of all the skeletal ghosts
lingering in the fleshy shadows
of unresolved affection.

- Happy Triggers

Pain is the absorption
of physical resolution.
When the soul, mind and
body are in desperate need
of the orgasmic sensation
of climaxing when fucking
the attractive vigor of life.
Fear, is the absorption
of emotional resolution.
The trigger of successful
happiness.

- Sci-Fi Underwear

I used to be quick
to board trains that
traveled along derailed
tracks of past love affairs.
Until the morning you
pulled up in a stolen
sports car flaunting
hot food, brown eyes
and sci-fi underwear.

- Neon Kisses

I want
to kiss you
beneath neon
doorways
in the rain.
After bribing
all of the Gods
to use the stars
as letters to spell out
your name.

- Dog Fights

We are a couple
of dogfighting airplanes
trying to rendezvous
for dinner at nine.
A pair of dried up
old bloodstains
washed out
with wine.
Refusing
to fade.
Insulting
time.

- Ceiling Stars

Velcro stars
on bedroom ceilings
are used as silly reminders
of life's removable beauty.
Designed to hijack the mind,
encouraging the dreamer
to become a permanent
ripple in time.

-Pyromaniac

I burn homemade
rye candles inside
of cardboard forts.
While I typewrite
drunk romance
novels in hemp
checkerboard
shorts.

- Main Event

Disappear to my place.
Dream beneath my sheets.
Hide behind my arms.
Smile against my heart.
Your happiness is my duty.
Come, sunflower.
Let me showcase
your beauty.

– Giant Peaches

As kids, he would
build her foreign
sandcastles
on local beaches.
As teens, they warred.
Engaging in violent sieges.

As adults, they cheated
and cheated. Living via
bullshit figure of speeches.

As lovers, they retired
in a sandcastle mansion
spanning across foreign beaches.
Where the trees touched the skies
and grew giant peaches.

- Latex Aroma

I'm addicted
to the sweet acid
that sweats through
your skin during sex.
A fatal mixture of soul,
honey, wax and caramel
scented latex.

- Chewy Cashews

Fictitious firehouses on fire.
Stripper gypsies in the streets
spreading love to inspire.
Broken monuments.
Severed statues.
Stale bread.
Chewy cashews.
My reality has become
an exiled imagination.
Dying in a distorted
universe with poor
circulation.

- Space Robots

Become a psycho
within the realm of nature.
Or become another robot extra,
acting among the terrestrials
beneath the zodiac stars
of Ursa Major.

- Reasons To Live

I hope the universe
provides you with acres
for your happiness.
Extra long dawns
for your extra
cute crankiness.
A non-fictional future
for your inconceivable
arts and crafts.
Fire and roses for your
unspeakable past.
I pray humanity
offers you reasons
to love, reasons to live
and all of the above.

- staring at speakers

I stare into inanimate speakers
hoping I can magically witness
the visuals of the static sound.
The same way I stare into the
uninhabited universe hoping
to physically witness the
answers that surround.

- Motto

Within our endlessly looping,
colliding kaleidoscope-shaped
universe. Energetic particles
dissipate the radiant poetry
of the cosmos, while human
intelligence has been racing
to rapidly evolve in order to
translate the those time
traveling poetic
mottos.

- super salty

If raindrops
are like poems,
I have written
you oceans.

- Balance

Let's fall in love
so I can turn
you into
poetry.
But not
for long
because
heartbreak
is poetry diplomacy.

Toast to Mom and Freddie

Every action has its equal opposite reaction. Thanks to Freddie smith our family once again has traction. You may drive trucks for a profession but our mother is your passion. You smack each other in the face with love, a true attraction.

We get our satisfaction
knowing your love is
everlasting. The way
he opens doors and
treats her like a
queen is tasking.

Yet he never falters, always giving, never asking. The only tears you ever give are from hysterically laughing.

Mom loves her walks. Freddie loves his napping. But when it comes to love, both parties involved are captain. You hoist each other higher than the peaks of misty mountains. Your knot has been tied a second time, you're now Eternal spouses.

The Poetry Kitchen

Part Three

Stormy

- Succulent Souls

She,
is a slithering,
shape-shifting serpent.
Synthesized in the shadows
of a scandalized Salem.
Scientifically engineered
by romantically inept
yet intelligent trolls.
One must behold
her malevolent
gallery of
succulent
souls.

- Bostonian

She's got those eyes
that scream adventure.
A fiery smile and body
of pure architecture.

Hidden tattoos of stars
from different skies.
A student of travel.
No strings, no ties.

An intelligent stoner
whose lungs are green
and soul, a rich blue.
A lover of puppies and
of course kitties too.

Her home is hidden
within the skyline.
A heart that bleeds
for Boston.

A heart of mass devotion
that will never be exhausted.

- violent violin

She
attached
titanium strings
to my leather heart
with staples and nails.
Tuned it to perfection
Then auctioned it for sale.

- Pedicures

You slay me with your gorgeous personality.
Blooming smile and hypnotic sexuality.
Ravishing hair and radiant curves.
Multicolored pedicures
and psychedelic
nerves.

- Sex Grease

Let's set the stage
with last night's bedsheets.
The ones we stained with wine,
blood, honey and sex grease.

- Fossils

I hide you in between
the chapters of my
imaginary novels.
Carving your face
out of the words.
Immortalizing
you as literary
fossils.

- Cosmic Bullshit

I used to watch the stars dance
within our overcrowded galaxy.
Wondering and studying their
immunity from gravity.
Curiously wandering
through the shadows
of the moonlight.
Deciphering the codes
left behind by the starlight.
Yet tonight I watch the same stars
as they dance against the blue.
But instead of cosmic bullshit,
all I can think about is you.

- Immortal Ideas

Humans don't live forever.
So spend the idea of forever
with the humans who want
to spend their mortal time
sharing the same
immortal idea
as you.

- Snapchat

We're moon people, you and me.
A couple of naked stars making
love above the seven seas.
Manipulating waves.
Enchanting human
moods. Maybe we
are the cause
for all of the
disappearing nudes.

- Paint by Numbers

I once tried to
paint you by numbers.
But I failed because I made
the foolish mistake of thinking
your beauty could be contained by
simple borders and colors.

- Book Nerd

My best friends of late
have been the characters in my books.
Mainly the bad guys, villains and pirates
with hooks. The whores, the thieves
and murderous cooks.

- How To Breathe

Suffocate yourself
in life so you can learn
the art of living in death.
A practice that will transcend
the essence of your every breath.

- Sandy Ass

May there always be sand
at your feet and a tangerine
horizon in your future.
Become nature and remove
your eyes from the computer.
May your heart always be stuffed
and your soul brimming with humor.
I hope your eyes catch fire
and body turns lunar.

- Someone Else

She loved him
when he told her
she was the center
of his attention.
The heart-shaped
bullseye of his
distorted vision.
Then she left him
once she found out
that the corners of
his eyes were not
meant for her, but
for the ghost of
someone else.

- Weird 1st Dates

I would
rather you
creep me out
on the first date
with your weirdness
and strangely humorous honesty
than to force feed me lies and smiles
to ease the nerves which comfort me.

- Abstract Spider

You're the spider
hiding in the corners
inside the chambers
of my vacant heart.
Spinning cyanide
silk, slowly
turning
me
into
abstract art.

- Empty Doorways

I
keep
seeing your
damned silhouette
lingering in empty doorways.
I keep mistaking you for the ghosts
which linger in the shadows
of my mind's hallways.

- Crash Site

We seemed to be firing on all cylinders.
Unfortunately, no one noticed
the damn sycamore.

- Lick the sky

Dominate
all tasks which
lead to advances
in self-intelligence
An educated mind is
a formidable weapon
of conscientiousness.
In this life, we are all
stargazing trees of flesh
with a soul and face.
Now sever your
branches
until
you're
roots start
to melt and
your crown
tastes space.

- Souvenir

You left home
in search of love
with a passport
and bookcase.
Now you
have
returned
with bats
in your heart
and vultures
in your suitcase.

- Laughing and Farting

I need a lady
I can kiss every hour.
A woman who laughs and
farts back when I fart
in the shower.

- Naked Hot Dogs

Naked hot dogs expose the size of the buns.
While corporate pit-bulls disguise the size of
the funds. Homeless humans are murdering
just for crumbs. Hungry hippos, the animals
we've become. Flesh and bone with an itsy-
bitsy skeleton. I am just a silver spider
hitching rides on gray elephants.
Poisonous ambitions dipping
white fangs into Intelligence.
My brown skin is bruised
from all the pangs of
this pestilence.

- Illusive Excuses

When confessions
become excuses
for obsessions
becoming abusive.
Love becomes illusive
and the truth, inconclusive.

- Flavorful

I just want to use my tongue
to create poetry below your waist.
For any good poet knows every
good poem begins with taste.

- Human Nails

Rain
bears witness
to all of man's
abominations.
The dead lay moist
in a seedless hibernation.
Cleansing the evils.
Drowning the veils.
Time becomes a coffin
hammered shut
with human nails.
Rain fears nothing
for its intelligence
is primordial.
Fear is a cosmic trait
inert in all things
extraterrestrial.

- Inward

Stop reaching
to the stars
above you
and start
reaching
into the
universe
within you.

- Domestic Opinions Matter

The biggest problem
in our 21st century utopia
is the vile idea implemented
by our righteous society,
that dreams are meant
to come second to
pleasing foreign
opinions.

- Foodie

Cataclysmic events
showcase the chaos
of nature's order.
The same way you
showcase your chaos
when I fuck up your
food order.

Brendan De Lucia

- Words on Walls

Walls of words
become windows
to randomized
dimensions.
Making poetry
the subconscious,
suspended connection
between human
and interstellar
perception.

- Sex on Stones

Beneath earth,
wax candles illuminate
the stalactites dreaming
above our bed of soft rock.
Allowing the magnetic pull
to undress us to the bone.
Inducing tremors to form
unnatural formations
within the stone.

- Deep Water

The hole in the hull
would normally alarm me.
But I am used to drowning
so imminent death
now calms me.

- Nuclear Love

You are a zombie super model
scuttling my gluttonous destroyers
attempting to flank love's hind-headquarters.
Weakened from heartbreak, my supply lines
fell to the mercy of your flak guns.
Without extraction I parachuted
blind into the center of
a nuclear reaction.
Falling prisoner
to the law of
gravitational
attraction.

- sandbox

You drew a line in the sand
and told me that this is
where my carnival ends
but it's also where
our adventure
begins.

- Emily 1/4

Your eyes are the designs
used for forging diamonds.
The split second shimmer
when the sun disappears
beneath the horizon.
Opal and oval
opportunities.
Oh how they
glow without
a hint of insecurity.

- Emily 2/4

Independent pearls of rare silver.
Kaleidoscope snow cones
with sprinkles of
turquoise glitter.
Circular paintings
of mid-winter sunsets.
Your deadliest weapons
yet most precious of assets.

- Emily 3/4

The depths of your eyes
provide enough space
to harbor my demons.
A pair of immortal roses,
forever blooming
regardless the
season.

- Emily 4/4

I have always been
a sucker for real magic.
But never one for the dramatic.
So I used modern day sorcery
to hang a photo of you from
my rear view mirror to
help soothe the
drama of
everyday
traffic.

\- Briny Photograph

Once upon a time,
I desired a land where
old stars became young candles and
father time swam among the fish, free.
Then I fell in love with you, a floating
photograph lost at sea. Dissolving
in salt and vitamin D.

- Seeing Red

Beware
of hollow
red organs
in soft hands...

...red hearts
are red flags.

- Brisk Froth

Refreshing sunshine
heats my under-caffeinated
morning coffee, while brisk winds
use their invisible hands to stir
the cream and sugar
until frothy.

- Freedom Naps

Freedom hides its programming
inside of cheap consumer coupons,
while flaunting its perks behind
retractable fast food windows
and unreasonably long naps
on leather futons.

- Rust > Makeup

I fancy a woman
with a little rust
on her antiques
over a fancy woman
with too much
concealer on
her cheeks.

Brendan De Lucia

- Room to Snuggle

My human hands
will never physically
be able to obtain the
moon above you. But
my mortal heart will
always make room
to love you.

- Horizontal Sanctuary

The horizon
always has
a horizon
of its own.
Which means
You and I still
have time to
float home
alone.

- Kissing Fire

Slaughter and burn
all existing and barely
breathing remnants of
your grieving past's journal.
Live today for tomorrow's future
or die in yesterday's untouchable
inferno.

- Time Machine

I can see everything
out of this magical
window of glass.
Everything new
is a broken down
time machine of
yesterday's past.
I'm precisely spinning
out of alignment.
A flesh and bone,
living, breathing,
dying advertisement.
Silently slipping
into new realms
of new worlds.

- Bacon and Eggs

I have never seen true fireworks until the night
I saw your eyes react with the moonlight. I
have never heard the magic of music until
the evening you whispered your secrets. I
have never known compassion until
the morning you spilled your heart
all over my bacon and eggs. I have
never felt balance until that long
weekend when we first held
hands. I have never known
love until you left us all
behind. But then I found
love, the truest of the
kind. The love I had
inside myself. The
love I thought
was always
blind.

- Plot Losers

Do not write stories
about people who
can't turn pages.
They will never
understand the plot,
therefore never fulfilling
the needs of your ending.

- Oral Traditions

I am tortured by
immortal fingernail moons.
Haunted by tiny floating airplanes
and brainwashed by social media.
Yet I am also a descendant of
tyrannical Kings and ancient
encyclopedias.

- Recycle

Mental confidence
is the most attractive
physical attraction.
Along with a healthy sense
of humor, a backpack
of magic and someone
who can recycle plastic.

- Bone Parties

The skeletons of
all the monsters I have
stored beneath my bed,
have all been forged into
labyrinths of confidence
inside of my head.

- Hitchhiking 66

I traded in my faith
for ammunition.
Car keys for rifles
and sanity for vision.

Money for maps.
Thoughts for facts.
Jewels for bait,
honey and traps.

Cellphone for a compass.
Love for numbness.
I surrendered my soul
and followed the
trumpets.

- Silver shit

Maneuver your bones
through the fleshy shadows
of reality's lifeless and wretched
nightmare. Beware the timely turret
and become a soul of gold within this
priceless world of decrepit silverware.

- Black Tie

My demons
hide behind
the beauty
of handmade
Geisha masks.
Disguised in suits
and ties, skirts and dresses.
They have these eyes
that know my sins
and lies that can
clean my messes.

- Trust

The man with the banjo
told me to trust the Earth.
The man with the rifle
told me to trust my resolve.
The man with the book
told me to trust the words.
The man without eyes
told me to trust the art.
Now I must convince
the man in the mirror
to trust his heart.

Part 4

---

weightless

- Not Silver

I thought I would hitchhike
the dangerous road your heart.
I prefer to travel at twilight.
After falling asleep
beneath the silver
stars in my
skylight.
You are
the broken
headlights of
my dreams. The
not so silver lining
tearing at my seams.

– Bare Naked Necessities

I keep razor blades
in my leather wallet
in case my finances
refuse to profit.

I keep a target on my back
for all the misconstrued logic.
I keep bullets with the names
of the creatures who threaten me.
I am living to keep nothing but
my bare naked necessities.

- Monsters in Pajamas

Phantom assassins
have infiltrated the
private opera of my
lucid dreams.
Educated demons
exploiting the silence
of my gruesome screams.
Subconscious monsters
playing pianos in pajamas.
Psychos in bandanas
laying siege with
heavy cannons.
Altering my
alchemy.
Incurring
heavy famines.

- Coffee Addicts

I witnessed a murder between the bookshelves.
A raging fire ignited by failed negotiations
between Dwarves and Elves. Magic spells
oozed from the crispy pages. Sea salt
filled the air, fighting for space
against famous apparitions
with twisted faces.
Dinosaurs in biker
leather searching
for long-lost,
cursed pirate treasure.
Knights in not so shining-
armor collected the heads
of the handsome Princes in
guillotines. This library, now a
warring submarine, has turned
timeless books into time machines
for all who fancy addictions to coffee beans.

- Suicide Awareness

Follow the razor blades
to the crimson pools
of reconciliation.
The empty pill
bottles to the
cold bodies
of depression
and misunderstood
gender identification.
We must remember the
single gunshots of the lost,
forgotten and traumatized.
Suicide is a festering intelligence
awaiting a damaged mind to infiltrate
and hypnotize.

- Eternal Life?

I have become too successful
at locking away my problems
in imaginary vaults inside
of invisible castles.
Maybe it's because
I continue hiding
my secrets within the
seeds of poisonous apples,
sprouting trees of mystery
to provide my lies with
enough oxygen to
outlive history.

- Maple

Moonshiners babysit
my juvenile intentions.
While my body disembarks
into intoxicated dimensions.
Gasping for toxic air beneath
the persuasion of the Devil's knees.
Bootleggers siphon my blood
like maple syrup from
maple trees.

- Peach Tree

Evolution,
has extinction level power.
Holding dominion over all species.
So while the universe continues
expanding and degenerative
human intelligence
inevitably increases.
Our atoms will evaporate,
dissolving us all to pieces.
But time is on our side, so
for now go plant your peaches.
Then meet me at our castle for our
glorious end on sandy beaches.

- Walls

If walls could talk,
would they laugh?
Would they lie?
They are embedded
with history and truth.
They've absorbed
pain and pleasure.
Witnessed violence.
Housed villains and
protected the innocent.
Some belong to homes
and others to institutes.
Would they speak fluently?
Would the language sound familiar?
Press your ear...what do you hear?

- Castle

I stumbled across her mending old paper cuts
she thought had healed. A once blooming flower,
now withering in bloody soil...ravished, lost
and peeled. Lounging on the front steps of
a forgotten castle, she nonchalantly sipped
brown liquor from a clear vile kept within
her crocodile satchel. Bleeding out from
a sizable hole in the center of her chest
while her nervous system was dying
for circulation, I stepped inside of
the castle only to find her heart
replacing a missing tabletop
globe stabbed with red
roses in very specific,
different locations.

- Happy Family

The evolution
of a happy family
can sometimes be found
fading away in forgotten file
cabinets in the basements of
rundown courthouses.

While the history of heartbreak
can often be traced back to
abandonment issues being
resolved in the basements
of whore houses.

- Cereal

At the dawning
of intelligence,
wisdom began
documenting
its happiness on
highly flammable materials.
Now the modern-day terrestrial
has to do their best job interpreting
the charred documents, causing over
stocked shelves of highly-saturated cereals.

- Fat Belly

We are all cosmic vessels of organic energy
and memories. In love with violence, sex,
heartbreak and creating enemies.
Conscious stones of flesh and
bone, destined to make
ripples. Desperate
children in dire
need of nutritious
milk from Mother
Nature's nipples. Addicted
to siphoning radiation from the
immortal tit of our timeless universe.
Animals and kingdoms. Extroverts and
introverts. We are too old to know the past
and too young to see the future. We are
crippled intergalactic gladiators who
fancy dying by excessive sugar and
wasting away in front of
intelligent computers.

- Neon Nightclub

I am not fond of neon nightclubs
or watered-down bars. Nor do I
enjoy courting divorced queens
and their promiscuous daughters
while the single kings practice
their intimidation tactics
across the dance floor as
failed fathers. I would
prefer to dance alone
on soggy parquets
amidst foggy
waters.
(Acoustic instruments only!
So the hideous creatures
can court the horny monsters.)

I am a simple man
with simple feelings.
For I prefer finger painted
closet doors and Christmas lights
dangling from bedroom ceilings.

- Land and sea

Let this forgotten shore of
rock and sand remind you
that life is but a salty
ocean in love
with
land.

-Dawn 1/2

Dawn reminded me
of my date with the grass.
Morning seminars with the
sun, discussing the nature of coffee
beans while waiting for time to pass.
Garden snakes are welcomed intruders.
Chewing on the wires of all my computers.
I prefer the company of dirt and funny shaped
insects. Odd sounding birds and weirdly
scented incense.

-Dawn 2/2

Broken guitars that almost sound just right.
Songs about the stars I can sing all night.
Falling in love on remote bridges where
the hidden rivers keep our secrets.
Casting stones as wishes while
snacking on peanuts.
Windows down,
bathing suits
on with you
as my
passenger.
Black shades,
open roads and the
burning of all calendars.

Freedom is you.
Freedom is me.
Freedom is loving the
Earth and loving the sea.

- Ranch

I will always make sure

there is ranch for the pizza.

Blankets for the bed.

Weed for the bong.

Pillows for your head.

Radiators on.

For tonight and every night,

I will be your home.

– Ice Cream

Love is music.
A commitment to beauty.
The bonding of body and soul.
Love is Neapolitan ice cream.
A dedication to balance.
The connection of
mouth and bowl.

- Slanted Proportions

My eyes are broken windows.
Riddled with distortion of
imperfect proportions.
So I use the warps and
slants to visualize all
of the important
portions.

- Dragon Teeth

I am among friends once the beasts of myths
welcome my mat with muck from their
hooves, paws and claws. All hats,
cloaks and capes are to be hung
from the dragon teeth affixed
to the mounted jaws. A
sacred place where we
can all fix our
flaws.

- Rocket Fuel Station

In a forest of dead trees,
you are the lone baby evergreen.
The place UFO's go to fuel
their space machines.

- Afraid of the dark

Sunshine, is the nickname
I have decided to give you.
It is the perfect protection
against the diminishing
blue.

- Wise man

Being human means
we are Earth's most
menacing predators.
This causes my attractions
to biologically prefer the
company of insects over
illuminating conversations
with environmental developers.
...
and all other species
of Homo Sapiens.

Brendan De Lucia

- Vinyl Dreams

Asleep on the bus,
scents of strangers
create the environments
of my city dreams.
Thirty awkward
conversations.
Thirty ear-bud
muted screams.
Sixty bodies dancing.
A hundred boots advancing.
A thousand mirrors glancing.
A witch in tow entrancing.
Awakened by the arrival.
Senses tuned in to survival.
My eyes open wide upon
the ending of the vinyl.

- Fishy Fishy

Let's go fishing for happiness
and see if we get a bite.
Smiles enjoy stars, so
the best time to
cast a line will
always be
at night.

-Juicy Succulence

Mountain peaks consume
rain clouds for sustenance.
Because deep rooted dreams
require the constant absorption
of elevated consciousness.

- Beautiful Ratios

I consulted a renowned painter
about commissioning a portrait
of you during the sunrise's
golden glow. He became
angry, calling me a
blind fool and
proceeded to
kick me out
of his studio.
Clearly, human
talent cannot replicate
your beautiful ratios.

- Sugar Stars

Red eyes,
I walk with
the light of Venus.
Skin of a human.
Heart of a Phoenix.

Eyes white with lies
break me down.
Red eyes build
me up.

My best friends in the
universe are the swirling,
sugar stars inside of my
morning coffee cup.

- Ghostly

You are snowflakes
under streetlights
at midnight.
A poltergeist
of moonlight.
Searchlight.
Crash site.

- Happy Curves

I want to be your
private obsession.
Your perverted secret
and personal collection.
I want to be the guy that
only makes your mouth curve
in the upwards direction.

- Wreckage

We are footprints in snow.
An abandoned car on
the side of the road.
A yellow glow.
Angels in red.
A missing toe.
Arrowheads.
Mistletoe.

- Jealous Dentist

I walked in on our toothbrushes again.
The ones I keep stored separately.
Then, something strange.
A moment of jealousy.

- Paint Night

Their love began
as emerald and crimson
squares during a couples
paint night of a numbered
moonlit dinner and ended
on the night they tripped
over their lies, spilling
buckets of paint
thinner.

- Buttermilk Silk

Gap toothed monsters with silk scales
navigate my cerebral ship of cacao timber
and buttermilk sails through coconut seas of
suicidal swimmers with river monster tails.
I am stuck somewhere between hunger
and desperation, balancing mind and
body on all-natural scales made
from contaminated
vegetation.

- ugly Rose

To the ugly seat on the train,
which all strangers try to avoid.
You are the beautiful rose
amidst the filth of the
rich, middle-class and
unemployed.

- Rock Life

Throw a rock and watch
as I ripple toward the sun.
But a rock is all I am.
Beneath the moon.
Being spun.

- Wild Things

We made love in the rainforest
so we could educate the
wild things in the wild
things we humans
enjoy enjoying.
To prove our
passion for
intimacy
as a species.
To prove that
we are capable of
more than just destroying.

- Horses and saddles

We gathered our gold in fake leather satchels.
Scattered our silver throughout black-
market raffles. Pawned off our
copper for amber cut castles.
Traded our water for oval
shaped capsules.
Exchanged all
of our axles for
horses and saddles.
We bartered our privileges
for pathways more primitive.
We are desperately tired of living
like limited citizens. So we decided to die
in the pursuit of becoming limitless pyramids.

- Heels

I murdered the coward
who's been hitchhiking
back and forth through
crimson nerve endings
from my head to my heart and
all the way down to my heels.
I committed this murder so
it would stop hurting to feel.

- Poetry

I write poetry because I can't afford therapy.
I write poetry because I cannot afford therapy.
I write poetry because I can't afford therapy.
I write poetry because I cannot absorb empathy.

- Friend of Old

In the basement,
hid the treasure.
A wooden casket and
a leather ledger.

Mummified dreams
hung from spider webs.
Mummified screams,
sang from shrunken heads.

The shelves were putrid,
drenched in black mold.
The lair of a gambler,
my friend of old.

Break into his house!
Is what I was told.
A mission to steal,
his guns and his gold.

All of this I was told from afar
by a weary old man at the bar.
With one one too many scars.

- Moldy Cavities

When you don't fit the mold, let yourself melt
into unfamiliar spaces until the voids start to
bend and twist themselves into perfectly
fitted threads that match your newly
shaped grooves...Our earth keeps
changing yet the planet
never moves.

- Balloon

Paper planes
can have engines
if you fold them right.

LOVE like a balloon
and hold it tight.

— All Life is bacteria

If we continue to grow and face the sun,
the unmeasurable potential is
achieving everything you
feared could never
be done.

\- Chickens

Decorated histories.
Lost and abandoned mysteries.
Humans are just chickens stuck inside
of Earth's rotisserie.

- Corny

I can't take my eyes off of you,
so I will replace them with mirrors.
This way, my soul's purpose will be
to reflect your beauty.

- supercharged sailboats

When we sleep,
our subconscious
drifts into dimensions
our conscious selves can't
yet comprehend . Which is why
we can travel to the future. The past.
Do impossible things. Dreams are just
supercharged sailboats with airplane engines,
built to venture to the spaces in-between spaces.

- spiders

Pretty humans
will always terrify spiders.
But, if spiders were pretty,
would you no longer
fear their nature?
To fear a monster
is simply
universal
behavior.

- Venice

I thought I found love
at two in the morning
on a beach in Venice.
Her accent, Italian.
Copper skin and
eyes a forest
blue. Turns
out, she was
just a tourist
too.

- Giant Diamonds

When the world
seems narrow and empty
and telescopes no longer
reveal those mysterious
cosmic diamonds.
Remember that the
stars were once dust
and humans were
once giants.

- Rainy Day

You are
my favorite
kind of weather.
My ultra fuzzy blanket
and my extra furry sweater.
My go to brand of chocolate
chip cookies and my treasured
collection of classic Disney movies.
My most beloved recipe.
My secret stash of
emergency ecstasy.
Sunflower, you
are my all time
favorite rainy
day necessity.

- Bird Divorce

Birds don't use
words to communicate
their love for one another.

They sing!

Bird divorce?
There is no such thing.

- Weirdo

I hoard microscopic portraits
of your biologic face inside of
semicircle chocolates
on plastic appetizer
plates.

- Infantry Elephant

My life has been a hallway
of gray-based masterpieces.
Oh so lifelessly elegant.
But, it is now time to
unleash the beautiful,
pigmented human I
was illustrated to be
and ride free into
the blazing sunset
atop my infantry
elephant.

- Foxy Bees

Silent trees.
Armored boats.
Foxy bees.
Briny moats.
Hippie snakes.
Racist assholes.
Shifty shapes.
Peasant castles.

Brendan De Lucia

- Travel Bug

Pack light
so you have
enough room
to bring back
new experiences.

- Mermaids

The air is thick
with low tide and
the rotten stink
of divorced flesh.
Beasts disguised
as humans all
dressed in the
same blood-
stained dress.
Seagulls begging
for bus fare with neck
ties tied around broken
necks. Blond surfers
maneuvering through
gray fins in waves
of crimson slaughter.
I am sick of the
Atlantic and her
mermaid-less
waters.

- Botany

Her cellar is overflowing
with candles, flesh, mold and ants.
Her pantry is crammed with
cookie dough, trash bags
and rare wine from France.
While her bedroom is filled
with the reincarnated bodies
of her exes disguised as plants.

- Black Soldier 1/2

Cornerstones were laid to prepare
the foundations for surpassing
unimaginable levels of
extreme elevation.

While dark skinned
humans laid down their
stolen bodies in an unfair fight
for the daydream of salvation.

Black soldier, spoon fed hearty lies
cooked into processed truths while
white leaders preached on about
" anything is possible ".

Black soldier, fought to die for this country
while being given improper drugs to feel
the rich power of being unstoppable.

Injured black soldier
with foreign bullets wedged
behind the clavicle, homeless,
begging for change on a rundown
bicycle; hunting for fifteen cheeseburgers
and a milkshake to stay fed through tomorrow.

When the fight is for food, freedom and the right
to work, the oppressed must commit treason in
the eyes of the righteous for it to work.
Inferiority is a term coined by insecure
people who are horrified of unification
and terrified of being equal.
The capacity of privilege
must not be allowed to
dictate segregation.
Every human has
a heart and every
person is the
product of
migration.

Thank you.

For Reading.

The End.

Brendan De Lucia

You can follow my work via social media
@Word. Bender

The Poetry Kitchen

Brendan De Lucia

Lightning Source UK Ltd.
Milton Keynes UK
UKHW021927290621
386378UK00008B/355/J

9 781006 809156